70 Sacrament Starters for CHILDREN

...and those who teach them

Patricia Mathson

TWENTY THIRD 23rd
PUBLICATIONS

Third printing 2012

TWENTY-THIRD PUBLICATIONS
A Division of Bayard
One Montauk Avenue, Suite 200
New London, CT 06320
(860) 437-3012 or (800) 321-0411
www.23rdpublications.com

The Scripture passages contained herein are from the *New Revised Standard Version of the Bible*, copyright ©1989, by the Division of Christian Education of the National Council of Churches in the U.S.A. All rights reserved.

ISBN 978-1-58595-645-6
Library of Congress Catalog Card Number: 2007930534
Printed in the U.S.A.

CONTENTS

INTRODUCTION

The seven sacraments are all about being Catholic! With signs, symbols, gestures, and prayers, we celebrate them as a Church and thus celebrate God's love and presence in our lives and in our world. The sacraments celebrate everything God has done in our lives and will continue to do. They give us hope, joy, and gratitude because they are signs of God's continuing presence among us.

The sacraments are an essential part of our faith journey. Through them we are called to express our faith in God who loves us with an unending love. The sacraments help us to live the challenge of the gospel and witness to the teachings of Jesus Christ. We are a sacramental people and catechesis on the sacraments is an essential aspect of lifelong faith formation.

As catechists and parents, we help our children learn that sacraments are not isolated moments in their lives, but are to be lived daily. Sacraments call them and us to give praise and glory to God. They help us to become all that we are created to be. We celebrate the sacraments within a church community because we need one another on our journey of faith. Each sacrament is a prayer of the whole Church. All of us of various ages and stages of life are called to give witness to the graces we receive through them. All of us are called to proclaim and share these gifts with our children.

This book will help children and their catechists and parents explore how to live the sacraments in their daily choices. The activities are for catechists in parish programs, teachers in Catholic schools, directors of faith formation, religion coordinators, family life ministers, leaders of lifelong faith formation, parents, grandparents, and all who minister to children and families. All of us must work together to help children of the next generation grow in faith, hope, and love of God and others.

The ideas here will work for both small and large groups (especially with children in grades one through five) and with groups in parishes and school settings. The ideas are family friendly and can be used when children and families come together in an intergenerational gathering or at home for family faith sharing.

There are a variety of activities here, including outreach projects, prayers, questions, crafts, posters, and gospel stories. Ten are offered for each of the seven sacraments. They are easy to do and require a minimum of preparation.

The sacraments draw us into our daily life with Jesus Christ and keep us focused on what is important. They call us to faith on an ongoing journey toward God who loves us with an unending love. They are signs of hope in our lives and our world today. As we share them with children, let us pray that they will be sacramental people, signs of Jesus Christ to all they meet.

BAPTISM

Sacrament of Belonging

Through the sacrament of baptism we share in the life that Jesus Christ gave us through his life, death, and resurrection. Baptism invites us to celebrate Christ's presence as a community of faith. It marks us with the sign of the cross as disciples of Jesus Christ.

We are baptized in the name of the Father and of the Son and of the Holy Spirit and thus called to life in the Trinity. Through our baptism we share in the mission of Jesus to proclaim the good news with others, to give witness to what Jesus said and did. Our baptism calls us to a way of life that includes both faith and action.

Catechesis for the sacrament of baptism is ongoing as we discover each day anew what it means to live as disciples of Jesus Christ. The following activities will help children to explore the sacrament of baptism more fully as part of their lifelong faith journey.

1

VISITING THE BAPTISMAL FONT

BACKGROUND

We are baptized with *water* in the name of the Father, Son, and Holy Spirit as a sign of life with God. All living things need water to live and grow.

We are anointed with *special oil* with the sign of the cross. This is to give us strength to live as disciples of Jesus in all we do and say. The anointing is an outward sign that we are marked for Christ.

We receive a *white garment* or wear one because we are a new creation in Jesus Christ through his life, death, and resurrection.

A *baptismal candle* is lit from the paschal candle. This symbolizes the light of Christ in our lives. During the rite the priest tells the parents and godparents to help the child walk always in the light of Christ.

WITH THE CHILDREN

Take the children on a trip to church to see the baptismal font. Display a candle and a white garment. Tell them where the oils are kept. Explore together the symbols of the sacrament of baptism—especially water, oil, a white garment, and light—to give the children visual reminders of their baptism.

Encourage the children to put their hand in the font and make the sign of the cross as a remembrance of their own baptism and as a promise to live as disciples of Jesus in their lives. Explain that each time we enter and leave the church we make the sign of the cross with holy water as a reminder of our baptism.

2 TALKING IT OVER

BACKGROUND

When we were baptized, our parents and godparents made "promises" in our name. They promised that we would follow the way of Jesus and reject the ways of Satan, and that we would accept the teachings of the Church (as described in the Creed).

WITH THE CHILDREN

Remind the children that promises were made for them when they were baptized which they renew at Easter and on other special occasions. The most important promise was to follow Jesus in all of their daily words and actions. Review this and other baptismal information through the following questions.

>> What is the first sacrament you received?

>> Why were you baptized with water?

>> Why is there holy water at the church doors?

>> Why did your parents light a candle when you were baptized?

>> How can you share the light of Christ with others?

>> Why do you have godparents? Who are they?

>> What does it mean to you to follow Jesus?

>> What are ways you can live your baptism every day?

Invite children to participate as you pose these questions, but remember that some children learn best just by listening to you and the other children.

3 CREATING A MISSION CROSS

BACKGROUND

At baptism you were asked to go out into the world and share the good news of Jesus Christ with others. Jesus Christ belongs to all people, all nations, and all cultures. As his followers, we are called to treat all people as our brothers and sisters. A mission cross can be a reminder of this.

WITH THE CHILDREN

Have each child cut out a large cross about twelve inches tall and eight inches wide using green construction paper. In the middle of the cross they can glue a copy of the Bible verse: "Love one another as I have loved you" (John 15:12).

Let the children select colorful pictures of people of many cultures from mission magazines or newsletters. They can cut out the pictures and trim them to fit on the cross. Each child needs five pictures to glue to the length and width of the cross. They should leave space between the pictures for best results. This makes a bright picture cross that will remind the children of the words of Jesus. They can display it at home as a reminder of their baptismal call to discipleship and to love others.

4 READING A GOSPEL STORY

BACKGROUND

Read together Matthew 28:16–20, the story of Jesus' appearance to the apostles in Galilee after his resurrection. He tells them to baptize others and give witness to what he has taught them. He promises to be with them always.

The risen Christ entrusts his mission to his disciples and to us. We are to continue the work that Jesus began through his earthly ministry. All of us are called to proclaim the good news of the gospel to others. We will not be alone because the risen Christ will be with us always. This passage proclaims that we are to make disciples of all nations. Jesus Christ came for all people. This includes all races, all cultures, and all nations.

WITH THE CHILDREN

Read the story from Matthew dramatically, if possible with different children reading parts of it. Then ask questions to review the story.

> » When did this story take place?

> » Where did the disciples go?

> » Who did they see there?

> » What did Jesus tell them?

> » Are we called to share the teachings of Jesus with others?

> » In whose name are people to be baptized?

> » When did Jesus say he would be with us?

5

SHARING THE STORY OF ST. PATRICK

BACKGROUND

The saints are people who imitated Jesus in their lives in many different ways. St. Patrick lived the gospel and did as Jesus commanded: to proclaim the gospel to others. St. Patrick traveled to Ireland and shared his Catholic faith with the Irish people. He went all over Ireland talking about God, baptizing the people, and building churches. St. Patrick taught the Irish people about the Trinity and led them to faith in God who is Father, Son, and Holy Spirit.

St. Patrick practiced the baptismal virtue of courage and he was a person of prayer. He heard God's call in his life. He is an example for all of us of living the gospel. We too are called to share the good news of Jesus Christ with others.

WITH THE CHILDREN

St. Patrick is best known for using a shamrock to demonstrate how there can be three persons in one God; there is one stem but three leaves on a shamrock. Invite the children to make green paper shamrocks using a pattern and a piece of green construction paper. If possible, give them shamrock stickers for each of the three leaves. Then they can write "Father," "Son," and "Holy Spirit" on each leaf. Conclude this activity by prayerfully making the sign of the cross.

6 CELEBRATING WORLD MISSION SUNDAY

BACKGROUND

Each year we celebrate World Mission Sunday on the second to last Sunday of October. As a worldwide Church, this is a time to recommit ourselves to proclaim the good news to others. We are called to be witnesses to the gospel and to God's love for each person. We are to bring to others the good news of Jesus Christ through the Holy Spirit who guides our Church and our efforts.

WITH THE CHILDREN

Missionaries carry the good news to people in our own country and in countries around the world. Sharing the good news is the responsibility of all of us. Encourage the children and families to contribute to the support of missionaries. Our donations and our prayers help support churches, hospitals, and schools in missions around the world. In this way we show others the love of God for all people.

7

RENEWING BAPTISMAL PROMISES

BACKGROUND

Remind children that when they were baptized, their parents and godparents made special promises for them. Invite the children to now renew their baptismal promises for themselves. This will help them connect the sacrament of baptism with their lives. Remind them that baptism calls us to share our faith and our gifts with others.

The promises that follow are adapted for children and do not include the full text.

WITH THE CHILDREN

Leader We are called by our baptism to live as disciples of Jesus Christ. We now renew the promises that were made for us at baptism. We declare our faith in the Trinity: Father, Son, and Holy Spirit. After each question, please answer "I believe."

Do you believe in God, the Father, who is the Creator of the world and everything in it and who loves us with an unending love?

Children I believe.

Leader Do you believe in the Son, our Lord Jesus Christ, who came to teach us how to live as we were created and to redeem us through his life, death, and resurrection?

Children I believe.

Leader	Do you believe in the Holy Spirit who lives in our hearts and who guides our Church and our lives?
Children	I believe.
Leader	As a sign that you will live up to your baptismal promises, you are invited to come forward and make the sign of the cross with holy water.

(*Children come forward*)

We now pray together the words that our Lord taught us as we give praise to God for all that God has done for us.

All	Our Father...
Leader	Remember that through our baptism we are called to share our faith in God with others. Each of us has God-given gifts to share with other people. We go now to love and serve God in all that we do.
Children	Amen.

8

WRITING ON
A HAND SHAPE

BACKGROUND

Our baptism calls us to be people of faith, hope, and love. We are to serve other people as Jesus was the servant of all.

WITH THE CHILDREN

Talk with the children about ways to reach out a helping hand to others, for example:

» being friendly to a new child in your school;

» helping an elderly neighbor;

» giving food to the food pantry;

» visiting residents at a nursing home;

» contributing to Catholic Relief Services;

» donating blankets to a homeless shelter;

» praying for the needs of other people.

After discussing these ways to reach out to others, personalize this message with the children by inviting them to make individual hand shapes. Have each child cut out a square of colored construction paper and trace his or her right hand on the paper. Ask each child to then write in the hand one way they will help others. Have them put their names on one of the corners and take home these hand shapes as reminders to care about other people.

9

SERVING OTHERS IN NEED

BACKGROUND

As disciples of Jesus Christ we are called to serve others as Jesus did; he was the servant of all. We are baptized into a way of life. Living out the sacrament of baptism means serving others. It is important to provide opportunities for children and families to serve others through projects that benefit people in the local community. One project is collecting the bare necessities that many of us take for granted. These are items we use each day, but can be hard to come by for people in difficult circumstances. Bare essentials include such items as soap, laundry detergent, paper towels, dishwashing liquid, shampoo, deodorant, toothbrushes, toothpaste, diapers, and baby formula.

WITH THE CHILDREN

Check with a local organization such as Catholic Charities about their specific needs. Once you know what they need, have children make posters about this project, inviting the participation of everyone in the parish or school. On their posters they can list the items needed and a date and place for receiving donated items. This project helps families to serve others in the name of Jesus Christ and reminds them that "giving" is a year-round necessity.

10

PRAYING A BAPTISM PRAYER

BACKGROUND

We must ask God's help to live up to the promises of our baptism. They are not light promises but rather are promises that demand our time, attention, and action.

WITH THE CHILDREN

Use the following prayer with the children, explaining that it sums up what they have learned about baptism.

Leader	God, Father and Creator,
Child One	We give you glory and praise today and always for all you have done for us.
Child Two	Help us to live up to our baptism by loving you and loving all people in your name.
Child Three	Enable us to be witnesses to your word in all that we do and to proclaim the good news of Jesus Christ to others.
Leader	May your Holy Spirit of love guide our lives and our hearts today and every day.
All	Amen.

CONFIRMATION

Sacrament of Witness

The sacrament of confirmation celebrates the presence of the Holy Spirit at work in our hearts and our lives. Through confirmation we receive a fuller outpouring of the Holy Spirit and are strengthened for following Jesus. Through the gift of the Holy Spirit in our lives we too are called to witness to all that we believe and to live out our beliefs in all we say and all we do.

All of us, whether we have been confirmed yet or not, are called to live Spirit-filled lives. We receive the gift of the Holy Spirit at baptism. Jesus promised to send the Holy Spirit to the apostles and he did that at Pentecost. The gift of the Holy Spirit reminds us that God is at work in our lives and our Church.

This sacrament "confirms" the promises we made at baptism and the life we are already living as disciples of Jesus Christ. Confirmation strengthens us for our faith journey. The coming of the Holy Spirit at Pentecost transformed the lives of the apostles and we too can be changed to live Spirit-filled lives.

Ongoing catechesis is important for the sacrament of confirmation so that we might live in the Holy Spirit each day, accepting the challenge of the gospel. We are to become all that God has created us to be. We are to lead Spirit-filled lives.

1

EXPLORING PENTECOST

BACKGROUND

At Pentecost the Holy Spirit came to the apostles and confirmed them in their faith in Jesus Christ. The coming of the Holy Spirit transformed the apostles from a group of frightened people who hid behind closed doors to people who courageously proclaimed the gospel. The coming of the Holy Spirit gave them hope and courage. We too can carry on the mission of Jesus Christ to the world with the help of the Holy Spirit.

WITH THE CHILDREN

Read with the children the story of the first Pentecost from Acts of the Apostles 2:1–4. Then read it again, this time with sound effects and gestures. These might include: noise of wind; making "V" shape over head (for tongues of fire); and arms outstretched (for bold proclamation).

2 LIVING IN THE SPIRIT

BACKGROUND

We are to live the sacrament of confirmation in our daily lives. Guided by the Holy Spirit we are able to be disciples of Jesus Christ. With faith, hope, and love, we are to witness to all that we believe. Confirmation helps us to do this. We carry on the mission of Jesus Christ to the world with the help of the Holy Spirit.

WITH THE CHILDREN

Discuss the sacrament of confirmation with the children using questions such as the following:

» Why do we renew our baptismal promises at confirmation?

» How does the Holy Spirit help us live as disciples of Jesus Christ?

» What does it mean to serve the poor?

» How can we stand up for the rights of other people?

» What can we do for the elderly?

» Why is going to Mass each week important?

» Is it easy to do the right thing?

» What does it mean to be people of prayer?

» How can we be peacemakers?

3 LEARNING FROM MOTHER TERESA

BACKGROUND

Mother Teresa's life showed what it means to live the sacrament of confirmation. She was first a teacher, but then she heard God's call to help the poor. She had the courage to change her life. She began to take in the forgotten people who were dying in the streets of Calcutta. She tenderly took care of them until they died. She washed them and fed them and talked to them. She dedicated herself to caring for the poorest of the poor. She saw the face of Jesus Christ in each person. Mother Teresa said that when a poor person dies of hunger, it is because we did not recognize Jesus Christ in them.

Mother Teresa lived the gospel every day. She began each day with prayer so that she would have the strength to do what needed to be done for others. We too are called to pray to the Holy Spirit for the courage and love to serve others each day. The followers of Mother Teresa are known as the Missionaries of Charity and still today care for the sick and dying around the world.

WITH THE CHILDREN

If possible, read the children a story about Mother Teresa or simply tell her story from the information above. Then invite them to write a prayer asking the Holy Spirit to make them strong enough to be good helpers—at home, at school, during activities—like Mother Teresa. Have them place their prayers in a special container and pray: "O God, you hear our prayers. We offer them to you with love." All respond: "Amen."

4 WALKING THROUGH THE RITE

BACKGROUND

Give children a brief overview of the rite of confirmation as it is celebrated in the Catholic Church. Review this first yourself by recalling the following rites.

Renewal of Baptismal Promises. At the time of our baptism promises were made in our name. At confirmation we make the baptismal promises our own. We state our belief in God who is Father, Son, and Holy Spirit, and in the Catholic Church.

Laying on of Hands. Each candidate comes forward with his or her sponsor. The bishop lays his hands on the candidate's head and prays that the Holy Spirit will guide their lives.

Anointing with Chrism. The bishop calls each candidate by his or her confirmation name as he traces the sign of the cross on the forehead of each person. They say "Amen" as a sign that they believe.

The rite of confirmation affirms that we are baptized Christians. We must witness to our faith in God in all that we do. We are to pray to the Holy Spirit to guide our lives always.

WITH THE CHILDREN

Invite children to role play these three aspects of the rite of confirmation. Have them take turns being the bishop, the candidates, and the sponsors.

5 MAKING A SPIRIT CROSS

BACKGROUND

It is important for all of us to remember to pray to the Holy Spirit to help us lead faith-filled lives. The Holy Spirit guides our hearts and lives.

WITH THE CHILDREN

By making a Spirit cross, children can better remember to pray to the Holy Spirit each day. Run off copies of small white doves and the words "Come Holy Spirit." Then each child can cut out a cross shape (nine inches by six inches) from a half sheet of red construction paper. The children can draw a decorative border around the edge of their cross. Then they can cut out the dove and the words and glue the dove in the middle of the cross with the words at the bottom.

Invite children to display their Spirit crosses at home as a reminder to follow the guidance of the Holy Spirit in their lives. The words on the cross call them to pray to the Holy Spirit often.

6 READING THE BIBLE

BACKGROUND

The role of the Holy Spirit in our lives is an important one. Look up and discuss the scripture citations below about the Holy Spirit. Remind the children that the promise of Jesus to send the Holy Spirit is a promise to us also.

» *God promised the people a new spirit.*
   EZEKIEL 36:26–28

» *The Spirit descended on Jesus.*
   MARK 1:9–11

» *Jesus promised to send the Holy Spirit.*
   JOHN 14:16–17

» *The Holy Spirit comes to us.*
   ACTS 1:8

» *The Holy Spirit has been given to us.*
   ROMANS 5:5

» *We share gifts in the Holy Spirit.*
   1 CORINTHIANS 12:4–7

» *We live in the Spirit.*
   GALATIANS 5:25

» *We are united in one Spirit.*
   EPHESIANS 4:1–6

WITH THE CHILDREN

Stress that the Holy Spirit who came to the apostles comes to us also. Talk about how each of us receives the gift of the Holy Spirit to help us live as disciples of Jesus Christ. Then have the children repeat each of the following lines after you:

» God promised the people a new spirit.

» The Spirit descended on Jesus.

» Jesus promised to send the Holy Spirit.

» The Holy Spirit comes to us.

» The Holy Spirit has been given to us.

» We share gifts in the Holy Spirit.

» We live in the Spirit.

» We are united in one Spirit.

CREATING POSTERS

BACKGROUND

As people who live Spirit-filled lives, we are to help those in need in our communities and our world. In the gospel of Matthew (25:34–40) we hear Jesus teach about the works of mercy. This gospel challenges us to see the face of Jesus Christ in others. Think about what the individual works of mercy mean and how you can live them in your life. The works of mercy in this gospel are: to give food to the hungry, drink to the thirsty, clothes to the poor, shelter to the homeless, to visit the imprisoned, and to care for the sick.

WITH THE CHILDREN

Read together Matthew 25:34–40. Explain that there are many people in need in our world. Discuss some of them including people who go to bed hungry at night, children with no access to clean water, refugees who must flee their country, elderly people who live in nursing homes due to ill health, children who do not have warm winter clothes to wear, and victims of discrimination.

To help them remember what Jesus said in this gospel, ask the children to work in small groups to make "works of mercy" posters. Have each group take a slip of paper bearing the name of one of the works of mercy and then design a poster based on this theme. They should write the work of mercy at the top with markers and illustrate the poster with pictures and symbols. Put the posters where the children will see them and be reminded that Jesus asks us to serve others in his name.

8 TALKING ABOUT CHOICES

BACKGROUND

The Holy Spirit helps us to follow the way of Jesus Christ. Through the sacrament of confirmation we are called to lead Spirit-filled lives. We believe that the Holy Spirit guides our hearts and lives when we must make choices.

WITH THE CHILDREN

Talk to the children about situations in their lives when they must choose to live in the Spirit. Use these scenarios as starters.

A refugee family moves into your neighborhood. They have fled because of war in their country. They do not speak your language well. What will you do?

One child tells a joke about people of another race. Everyone laughs. What will you do?

Your parish is having a collection of books for children in need. The books will be part of a children's library at a family shelter. But you love all your books. What will you do?

You said something to someone that wasn't very nice. You hurt their feelings. What will you do?

A new child doesn't have anyone to eat lunch with. You like to eat lunch with your friends. What will you do?

An elderly woman in your neighborhood has difficulty with chores. She does not get around very well. What will you do?

Guide the discussion as needed, but encourage the children to think of their own creative ways to complete these scenarios. Explain that one person really can make a difference in the life of someone else. Remind the children that they can call on the Holy Spirit to guide them when they need to make difficult decisions.

9

COLLECTING FOR AN AFTER-SCHOOL CENTER

BACKGROUND

As people of the Holy Spirit, we open our hearts to the needs of others. In many communities there are after-school centers for children in low-income families. These centers provide a safe place for children to go after school each day. Snacks, activities, games, and help with homework are part of the enrichment at such sites.

There is an ongoing need for supplies by the organizations that sponsor the centers. Many children participate in the activities. Items usually needed include markers, crayons, glue sticks, scissors, construction paper, drawing paper, notebook paper, pencils, pens, rulers, folders, games, jump ropes, puzzles, books, children's magazines, individually wrapped snacks, and napkins.

WITH THE CHILDREN

If you have such centers in your area, talk about them with the children you teach. Explain the need for supplies and provide a list and ask the children and their families to bring in items to be donated. In this way they will be reaching out with a helping hand to others—as the Spirit of love directs them to do.

10 PRAYING A LITANY

BACKGROUND

One way to pray to the Holy Spirit is with a litany that remembers the needs of others and our own needs. We pray that with the help of the Holy Spirit we may find a way to help people in difficult circumstances.

WITH THE CHILDREN

Invite individual children to read the following petitions. All the children can join in on the response. Following is a litany that calls on the Holy Spirit for those in need.

*Child
One* For the sick and the elderly, may they find comfort in the kindness of others, we pray...

All Come, Holy Spirit.

*Child
Two* For the poor and the homeless, may people learn to share what they have, we pray...

All Come, Holy Spirit.

*Child
Three* For victims of war and injustice, may our world learn to live in peace, we pray...

All Come, Holy Spirit.

*Child
Four* For our church, may we be signs of hope for others in our world today, we pray...

All   Come, Holy Spirit.

Child
Five   For all of us gathered here, may we live always with hearts filled with love, we pray...

All   Come, Holy Spirit.

Leader   Holy Spirit, fill our hearts with love for all these people and needs. Help us to reach out to those in need—as you call us to do.

All   In the name of the Father and of the Son and of the Holy Spirit. Amen.

EUCHARIST

Sacrament of Love

The Eucharist is a great and loving gift from God. Through it Jesus Christ fulfills his promise to be with us always. As Catholics when we say "Amen" as we receive Communion, we are saying that we believe that Jesus Christ is present in the bread and wine. It is as a community of faith that we celebrate the Eucharist.

The Eucharist calls us to give thanks to God who is the source of all good things. The word Eucharist means thanksgiving. Through it we gather together to give thanks to God for all that God has done for us. We offer to the Father the gift of the Son through the action of the Holy Spirit. The Eucharist gives us strength for our life journey and renews our hope in Jesus Christ.

In the Eucharist we are united not only with Jesus, but also with one another and with all people. Coming forward for Communion is our pledge that we will live as disciples of Jesus Christ. We believe in what he taught, including that all people are God's children. The Eucharist is at the center of our lives and our faith. Receiving it commits us to Jesus and to others, especially the poor and the vulnerable and those who have no one to speak up for them. The Eucharist challenges us to see Christ in others.

Following are some learning activities to help children and families grow in their understanding of the sacrament of the Eucharist and how to live it in their lives each day.

1 READING ABOUT THE LORD'S SUPPER

BACKGROUND

Explain that on the night before he died, Jesus shared a meal with his apostles. This was when he gave us the gift of the Eucharist so that he could be with us always. At the table Jesus took the bread and wine and gave it to his disciples as his body and blood. The words spoken by Jesus Christ at the Last Supper are proclaimed by the priest at every Mass as the bread and wine become the gift of Jesus Christ in the Eucharist.

WITH THE CHILDREN

Read together the account of the Last Supper in the gospel of Mark 14:22–24 or in one of the other gospels. Then explore the idea that at Mass we offer the gift of the Son to the Father through the Holy Spirit. It is through the action of the Holy Spirit that today the bread and wine at Mass continue to become the body and blood of Jesus Christ. Stress that Jesus Christ is truly present in the bread and wine although it still retains its outward appearance.

Ask and share answers to these questions:

» What were Jesus and his apostles doing?

» What words did Jesus say as he offered the bread and wine?

» What does the priest say at Mass at the consecration?

» When do we receive the body and blood of Jesus?

» What does it mean to be people of the Eucharist?

2 TAKING A CHURCH TOUR

BACKGROUND

The parish church is a place where we gather together to celebrate the Eucharist and give thanks to God for all God has done for us. A great way to explore the church is with a church search. This self-guided activity helps children learn about some of the items used for the Mass and its prayers and rituals. This can be done with pairs of children, an older child with a younger child, or with parents and their child.

Create a checklist of items in the church you want them to find. If there is something special in the parish church like a statue of the patron saint or a stained glass window, include that in the church search also. Before the church search make signs with the name and a short description of each item. Place each sign in an upright plastic sign holder and place it on or next to the location of the item.

As you will see, the church search gives children the opportunity to learn about their parish church, review difficult vocabulary, and get an up-close look at the items used at Mass.

WITH THE CHILDREN

Give each pair a checklist and a pencil. Pairs can go in any order they want. One child can read the description out loud at each place and the other can mark an X next to the name of the item on the checklist before moving on. Following are the descriptions that can be used for the church-search signs.

Altar. This is the table around which we gather to give praise and thanks to God at Mass.

Ambo. This is where the scriptures are proclaimed at Mass. We listen to the Word of God and try to live the message in our lives.

Baptismal font. We make the sign of the cross with holy water when we enter and leave the church as a reminder of our baptism.

Book of the Gospels. We hear stories about Jesus from the gospels of Matthew, Mark, Luke, and John. As Christians, we are asked to live the gospels in our daily lives.

Candles. The light of the candles reminds us to follow Jesus Christ who is the light of the world.

Chalice. The chalice holds the wine that becomes the blood of Jesus Christ at Mass through the action of the Holy Spirit.

Cross. The cross reminds us of how Jesus died and of God's unending love for each of us.

Paten. The paten holds the hosts that become the body of Jesus Christ at Mass through the action of the Holy Spirit.

Sacramentary. This book has the prayers that the priest says at Mass.

Sacristy. This is the room where the priest puts on his vestments before Mass. Items needed for Mass are also stored there.

Tabernacle. We genuflect before the tabernacle because Jesus Christ is always present there in the consecrated hosts.

Vestments. The priest wears these clothes when he celebrates the Mass. There are different colors for different seasons of the church year.

3 LOOKING UP GOSPEL STORIES

BACKGROUND

We are to live as people of the Eucharist each day. Look up and discuss gospel verses that show how to follow Jesus. The following are gospel stories that all of us should know and live as people of the Eucharist.

Our Father—MATTHEW 6:9–13

Rich man—MATTHEW 19:16–22

Take up your cross—MARK 8:34

Greatest commandment—MARK 12:28–31

Jesus calls the apostles—LUKE 5:1–11

Good Samaritan—LUKE 10:29–37

Love one another—JOHN 15:17

WITH THE CHILDREN

If possible give each child a Bible and invite each to look up the Scripture stories above. Another option is for the whole group to look up each story or the children can divide into small groups with each group focusing on one story. When they have found all the stories, ask each child or group to share from which story they learned the most about Jesus and how he wants them to live.

4 MAKING A HEART MAGNET

BACKGROUND

As people of the Eucharist we are asked to love others as Jesus showed us. By making the heart magnets with children, you are giving them a reminder to love others as Jesus did. Have available heart patterns and sheets of craft foam for this project.

WITH THE CHILDREN

Have each child cut out one large red heart and put a strip of magnetic tape on the back, with that side down. Next they can cut out smaller heart of a coordinating color and glue it on top. Invite them to display the hearts at home as a reminder to love others in the name of Jesus Christ. The hearts will stick to a refrigerator, filing cabinet, or other metal surface.

5

REVIEWING MASS RESPONSES

BACKGROUND

The Mass is the source and summit of our faith as Catholics. We cannot talk about the Eucharist without discussing the Mass. This activity encourages the children to actively participate in Mass each week and helps them review some of the Mass responses and prayers.

WITH THE CHILDREN

Focus on some of the simpler responses first, for example, "The Lord be with you." "And also with you." Have each child take a turn saying the first and all can respond as the congregation would.

Next focus on the responses to the readings: "The Word of the Lord" and "The Gospel of the Lord." Have each child say "The Word of the Lord" and all can respond, "Thanks be to God." Then have each say "The Gospel of the Lord," and all can respond, "Praise to you, Lord Jesus Christ."

If you have time, also talk about the "Gloria" and "Holy, Holy." Remind children that these beautiful prayers help us praise our God together and express what we believe as Catholics.

6 LEARNING FROM ST. KATHARINE DREXEL

BACKGROUND

The lives of the saints provide examples for us to follow. Saint Katharine Drexel had a great devotion to Jesus Christ in the Eucharist. She lived her faith by serving others and working for justice. She was born into a wealthy family in Philadelphia. As a child she followed the example of her parents in helping the poor. But people were shocked when this rich socialite decided to become a religious sister. Katharine was concerned about the poor and oppressed people in the United States, especially minorities. Her missionary work took her to various areas of the west and south. She was a generous person and used her entire inheritance to help others. She opened schools and missions for the poor and worked tirelessly for social justice and against racism.

It was a joy for Katharine to receive the Eucharist and to unite herself to Jesus in this way. This gave her strength to meet the challenges of each day. The last years of her life she was ill and spent her days in prayer.

WITH THE CHILDREN

Share St. Katharine's story and explain that her life reminds us to work for justice for all people of all races and to pray for people who live with discrimination. When we center our lives on Jesus in the Eucharist, we too will have the courage to reach out to others. Invite children to pray the following "litany" to St. Katharine and then to add spontaneous prayers of their own.

Leader	We pray, dear God, for all your children in need with St. Katharine Drexel as our guide.
Child One	That we may treat all people as brothers and sisters...
All	St. Katharine, pray for us.
Child Two	That we may share our clothes, toys, and money with those in need...
All	St. Katharine, pray for us.
Child Three	That we may share in the Eucharist often and receive the strength to help others...
All	St. Katharine, pray for us.
Leader	I invite you now to pray for your own needs and the needs of our world.

(*When all have prayed, exchange a sign of peace.*)

7

MAKING DOOR DECORATIONS

BACKGROUND

Talk with the children about living as Eucharistic people. Through the Eucharist they are united with Jesus Christ and with one another. Receiving the Eucharist is a commitment they will share with others, especially the poor and those in need. When they are sent forth from Mass each week, they are sent to live their faith in all their words and deeds.

We must provide opportunities for the children to reach out to other people. One great project for this is to make flower decorations for each resident's door at a local care center or nursing home. Find out in advance how many doors there are, so that each resident will have a decoration.

WITH THE CHILDREN

Show them how to cut out five large circles from pieces of colorful construction paper: red, green, orange, blue, or purple. Use small dessert size paper plates for patterns. These will be the flower petals. The children can also cut yellow centers for their flower and glue each petal in a circle around the yellow center. They should also glue each petal to the next petal. Be sure they put enough glue so that the flowers will stay together.

Later you can use masking tape to attach the flower decorations to the doors. This is a terrific project that brightens up the hallways at a nursing home and brings smiles to the faces of the elderly residents. If some of the children can accompany you, all the better.

8 DRAWING THE EMMAUS STORY

BACKGROUND

The Eucharist calls us to see the presence of Jesus Christ in scripture, in the bread and wine, and in one another. The story of Jesus and the two disciples on the road to Emmaus from the gospel of Luke (24:13–35) brings home this message. It reminds us that we too are disciples who are on a faith journey. As we go forth in life we are called to recognize Jesus Christ in the Word and in the Eucharist. In this way Jesus Christ is with us always.

WITH THE CHILDREN

Share this story by reading it slowly and dramatically.

Two disciples were walking along the road to the town of Emmaus. Suddenly they were joined by a person they did not recognize. This person talked to them about the scriptures as they walked along, and they were amazed at everything he knew. The disciples invited him to stay with them since it was getting dark. Then, when they all sat down to dinner, the man took the bread and broke it to share with them and all at once they recognized him. It was Jesus!

Now invite the children to draw a picture based on this gospel story. They can illustrate Jesus walking along sharing the Word with the disciples or Jesus breaking the bread with them. Provide paper and markers. Let the children use their creativity and their imaginations. When they are finished, invite them to share their pictures with the group. They can tell about their picture and what it shows and why they drew it the way they did.

9

ASSEMBLING A PRAYER CHAIN

BACKGROUND

As people of the Eucharist, we must remember to pray for others. If we receive the sacrament but do not share our lives with others, we are not allowing Jesus to work through us. Reaching out to others is a sign of our faith in and love for Jesus in our world.

WITH THE CHILDREN

Invite the children to make a prayer chain. Provide colorful construction paper and have them cut one-inch strips lengthwise down the sheet. On each strip they can write the name of a group or individual who needs their prayers. This can include the poor, the homeless, the hungry, the sick. It can also be a friend or neighbor who is sick or a family member who is in the hospital. Each child can make several prayer strips.

Next, show the children how to assemble a prayer chain by making a loop and securing it with scotch tape. Then they put the next strip through the loop and so on. The children should link all their prayer intentions together. Place the chain where all the children can see it as a reminder to pray for the needs of others each day.

10

PRAYING A EUCHARISTIC PRAYER

BACKGROUND

As eucharistic people, we know that we need spiritual nourishment to live as disciples of Jesus. Pray the following prayer before you gather with the children.

Jesus Christ,
*   we praise you as the Lord of all people.*
We thank you giving yourself to us
*   in a special way in the sacrament of the Eucharist.*
May we always give glory to your name
*   by the way we live our lives.*
May we remember that being one with you
*   means being one with all people.*
Help us to be bread for others
*   and serve them as you were the servant of all.*
May we live always as your Eucharist people. Amen.

WITH THE CHILDREN

Using the prayer above in a simplified form, pray it slowly with the children and have them do the gestures—as led by you.

Dear Jesus, (*folded hands*)

We are happy that you love all people (*hands on heart*)

We thank you very much (*arms spread wide*)

For giving yourself to us in Communion (*heads bowed*)

When we leave the church, please come with us
    (*"Come with us" gesture*)

So we can remember your words and deeds (*touch head*)

And try to help all those around us in need
    (*"reaching out" gesture*)

May we follow you always, dear Jesus (*walk in place*)

Amen. (*hands folded*)

RECONCILIATION

Sacrament of Forgiveness

The sacrament of reconciliation is a sacrament of forgiveness and mercy. Our God is a merciful and loving God. We know that God will always forgive us. This is the God that Jesus showed us through his words and actions. This sacrament is a sign of hope for us because we know that we can begin anew.

The sacrament of reconciliation which we celebrate as Catholics is an opportunity to take a look at our lives and where we are going. We must turn away from the selfishness of sin and toward the light of Christ. Sin is not just doing something wrong. It is also omitting to do something that might have made a difference in the lives of others. Through this sacrament, Christ continues to forgive our sins as he forgave people in his own time.

Through the sacrament of reconciliation we are reconciled to God and to one another. We must ask forgiveness of God and others for what we have done wrong and for what we have failed to do right. As God forgives us, so we must forgive others. We must grant forgiveness to other people even if they do not ask for it. We are called to act as reconcilers in our world.

It is important to provide ongoing catechesis for this sacrament because as we grow in faith, so will our understanding of forgiveness.

Following are some learning activities for children and their families. These ideas will help them explore the sacrament of reconciliation and how to live as reconciling people each day.

1

DISCUSS THE STORY OF ZACCHAEUS

BACKGROUND

The sacrament of reconciliation is a sacrament of conversion. We see this in the story of Jesus and Zacchaeus (Luke 19:1–10). Zacchaeus, like the other tax collectors of his time, often cheated people and stole from them. After his meeting with Jesus, Zacchaeus turned his life around. Jesus brought hope and forgiveness into his life.

WITH THE CHILDREN

Share this scripture story with the children. Ask them to pay special attention to the response of Zacchaeus to the presence of Jesus in his house. Zacchaeus says he will repay others. Explain to children that this story teaches us that we too must make up for the harm we cause by our actions and by what we fail to do. It is not enough to just say we are sorry. We must make up for the harm we have caused in any way we can. Also we have to resolve not to sin again. Encountering Jesus in the sacrament of reconciliation should bring about change in our lives as it did in Zacchaeus' life.

Use the following questions to encourage discussion and sharing with the children.

>> What job did Zacchaeus have?

>> Why did he climb a tree?

>> What did Jesus say to him?

>> Why did the people in the crowd grumble?

» Did Jesus come for all people?

» What did Zacchaeus say to Jesus?

» How can we make up for harm we cause?

» Why should our lives change because of Jesus?

» How does the sacrament of reconciliation help us?

2 EXPLORING BIBLE STORIES

BACKGROUND

Jesus Christ showed us that our God is a God of mercy, and that we should turn our lives away from the darkness of sin and toward the light of God.

WITH THE CHILDREN

Explore some of the Bible stories below about forgiveness. After each, ask and discuss the question that follows it.

Blessed are the peacemakers—Matthew 5:9

> ARE YOU A PEACEMAKER?

Repent and believe—Mark 1:14–15

> WHAT DOES IT MEAN TO REPENT?

Forgive so the Father can forgive—Mark 11:25

> IS IT EASY TO FORGIVE OTHERS?
> WHY OR WHY NOT?

Forgive seven times seventy—Luke 17:4

> HOW MANY TIMES IS SEVEN TIMES SEVENTY?
> WHAT DO YOU THINK JESUS MEANT?

Good Shepherd—John 10:11–15

> WHO IS THE GOOD SHEPHERD?

3

LIVE IN FORGIVENESS

BACKGROUND

It is important to provide children the opportunity for discussion about the concept of forgiveness. Let them know that we are to ask forgiveness of God for what we have failed to do right, as well as for what we have done wrong. We must also ask forgiveness from others we have hurt by our words and actions. We should make up for any harm we have caused others. We are also called to forgive others who hurt us even if they do not ask for forgiveness. We are not to hold grudges.

WITH THE CHILDREN

Invite children to gather as pairs to brainstorm situations that call for forgiveness. Ask them to talk it through carefully so they can role play their examples for the class. After each role play, ask other children what they would have done. Conclude this activity by praying for forgiveness together in these words:

Dear God,
We are sorry when we hurt others.
Please forgive us
And in the same way,
We will forgive those who hurt us.
Amen.

4

CREATING A STAINED-GLASS CROSS

BACKGROUND

As disciples of Jesus Christ we are to live in reconciliation and peace. Children need reminders to live their faith each day. One way to help them is to make stained glass crosses using construction paper. This craft allow the children to use their creativity and imaginations to create something to take home as a reminder to follow Jesus.

WITH THE CHILDREN

Show the children how to cut out a large cross (eleven inches high by eight inches wide) from a sheet of purple construction paper. Then have them cut one-inch squares from other colored paper: red, orange, blue, green, and yellow. No measuring is needed. They can use a glue stick to glue the squares to the cross in any arrangement they like.

5

WALKING THROUGH A RECONCILIATION SERVICE

BACKGROUND

Walking through the various aspects of a reconciliation service helps children understand what this sacrament means for Catholics. What they do and say helps them to be open to the forgiveness of God.

Introductory Rites. We gather together to celebrate that our God offers forgiveness and mercy.

Celebration of the Word of God. We listen to a Scripture story about forgiveness and reflect on what we have done wrong and how we have failed to live God's law of love.

Rite of Penance. We pray together asking forgiveness. Then we receive the sacrament of reconciliation individually from a priest. We confess our sins and the priest says a prayer of absolution. The priest also gives us a "penance" to do or say later. (A penance is a prayer or action that we do to show that we are sorry for our sinful actions.)

Concluding rite. We receive a blessing in the name of the Trinity, to live in peace with our God and with one another.

WITH THE CHILDREN

First explain to the children that they can also receive the sacrament of reconciliation as individuals. Share with them the regularly scheduled times available for receiving this sacrament in your parish. Then invite children to close their eyes and think about what they might say to God after receiving this sacrament. Ask each to think of one or two words and write these on a piece of paper. Then invite children to decorate their words.

6 LEARNING FROM ST. ANTHONY OF PADUA

BACKGROUND

St. Anthony is a great saint who believed in the importance of the sacrament of reconciliation. As a young man he decided to give his life to God and became a Franciscan priest. St. Anthony liked to read and reflect on scripture. One day he was asked to preach and everyone was amazed at how good a speaker he was. Soon big crowds gathered to hear him whenever he preached. He traveled throughout Italy and France teaching the people. He encouraged them to live the gospels and to follow Jesus Christ in their lives.

One of St. Anthony's greatest joys was helping people turn their lives around through the sacrament of reconciliation. As a Catholic priest he helped people reconcile with God and others through this sacrament. He helped them experience God's forgiveness in their lives. Many people waited for hours in long lines to receive this sacrament from him. He was a caring and compassionate person. His story reminds us that the sacrament of reconciliation is a gift in our lives.

WITH THE CHILDREN

Help the children see this sacrament as an opportunity to experience God's forgiveness in their lives. Talk about it as something they get to do, rather than have to do. God's mercy and this sacrament are a blessing to us.

7

ACTING OUT THE PRODIGAL SON STORY

BACKGROUND

This parable of the prodigal son is found in the Gospel of Luke 15:11–32. This story is really about the forgiving father more than the prodigal son. The father reaches out to welcome home the prodigal son as God our Father reaches out to us with forgiveness.

WITH THE CHILDREN

Read this parable with the children and discuss it. Talk about the Father who doesn't even wait for the son to get to the door. He goes out to greet him and forgive him. Remind the children that, like the younger son, they can always come home to God. God will always forgive them.

Spend some time also with the part of the story about the older son. Stress that the celebration for the younger son does not mean that the father doesn't care about the older son. But the older son is jealous and righteous and refuses to come to the party. We must remember that we cannot judge the actions of a forgiving God by our standards.

Then invite the children to act out the story as it is read from the Bible. Taking parts will help them understand the story and what it is about. The children can take turns playing the father, the prodigal son, and the older brother. This will help the story come alive for them. After the role playing ask: How did it feel to be the forgiving father? The prodigal son? The older brother?

8 BECOMING PEOPLE OF PEACE

BACKGROUND

A beautiful prayer, written in the tradition of St. Francis of Assisi, teaches us what it means to live as followers of Jesus Christ. It opens our minds and hearts to how we can live in love and peace each day and work for peace in our world. It's called the Prayer of St. Francis.

WITH THE CHILDREN

Give each child a copy of this prayer. Pray it together and then discuss what it means for them.

> PRAYER OF ST. FRANCIS OF ASSISI
>
> *Make me, O Lord, an instrument of your peace.*
> *Where there is hatred, let me sow love;*
> *Where there is injury, pardon;*
> *Where there is doubt, faith;*
> *Where there is despair, hope;*
> *Where there is darkness, light;*
> *Where there is sadness, joy.*
>
> *O Divine Master, grant that I may not so much seek to be consoled as to console; to be understood as to understand; to be loved as to love.*
>
> *For it is in giving that we receive; it is in pardoning that we are pardoned, and it is in dying that we are born to eternal life. Amen.*

Use questions to help the children reflect on this prayer.

» How can I be an instrument of peace? How can I "sow" love? Why is it important to treat people of all races and nations with respect?

» Does God want us to forgive those who hurt us? How do we know?

» Do our actions show Christ's love to people?

» How can we bring joy to the lives of others?

Encourage the children to pray this prayer at home.

9

WORKING ON PEACEMAKER POSTERS

BACKGROUND

All of us are called to live in peace in our neighborhoods, our country, and our world. We are to bring hope to others by working for peace and justice. Jesus said: "Blessed are the peacemakers" (Matthew 5:9).

WITH THE CHILDREN

Talk with the children about ways to live in peace, for example:

» show respect to people of all cultures and nations,

» defend the rights of others,

» forgive those who hurt us,

» write to politicians about the need for peace,

» do not return violence with violence,

» share what we have with others so they will have what they need,

» try to bring peace to people who do not get along.

Ask the children to assemble in small groups to make mini-posters (or 8.5 x 11 pieces of paper) about ways they can live in peace with one another and work for peace in our world. The title on each poster should be "Blessed are the Peacemakers." Put up the posters in a hallway or gathering space where they will be a reminder to live in peace to everyone who walks by.

10 PRAYING FOR RECONCILIATION

BACKGROUND

We should pray each day for the help of the Holy Spirit to be faithful to the way of Jesus Christ, which is a way of reconciliation and forgiveness. We are called to be people of prayer in all that we do. We should also ask forgiveness of God when we have not followed God's will.

WITH THE CHILDREN

Pray the following prayer with the children, but have them practice their parts before praying it all together.

Child
One Dear God, help us to be truly sorry for what we have done wrong and for the things we have not done to help others.

All Forgive us, dear God.

Child
Two We are sorry for the times when we have been selfish and turned against you and other people.

All Forgive us, dear God.

Child
Three May we remember that you always forgive us and always welcome us back.

All Forgive us, dear God.

Child
Four   Help us to ask forgiveness of those we have hurt by our actions and to make up for any harm we have caused to others.

All   Forgive us, dear God.

Child
Five   May we grant forgiveness to those who have hurt us as Jesus Christ taught us by his words and actions.

All   Forgive us, dear God.

Child
Six   Send your Holy Spirit to us that we may live always as reconciling people. Through you all things are possible.

All   Amen.

ANOINTING OF THE SICK

Sacrament of Compassion

Through the sacrament of the anointing of the sick, our Church follows the example of Jesus Christ who cared for the sick. The gospels tell many stories about the compassion of Jesus for those who were ill. He reached out to people who were mentally or physically ill. He healed people and cared about them.

The sacrament of the anointing of the sick comforts those who are sick and their families. It gives them hope that God is with them and gives them strength for the journey. Through this sacrament we pray with those who are sick and for them so that they will have courage in their time of need.

All of us are called to have compassion for the sick in the name of Jesus. We can reach out to people in ill health, those who are injured, in the hospital, facing long-term medical treatment, having surgery, are mentally ill, suffering from depression, living with a disability, elderly, and all those who are hurting in some way. In this way we follow the example of Jesus, who showed us what it means to live in love for others.

Ongoing catechesis for this sacrament reminds us to have compassion for others and help others as Jesus did. As a church community, as families, and as individuals, we must open our hearts to the needs of the sick in our communities and our world.

Following are learning activities that will help children and families learn about the sacrament of the anointing of the sick and give them ways to minister to the needs of the sick and elderly.

1

LOOKING UP GOSPEL STORIES

BACKGROUND

The gospels are filled with accounts of how Jesus Christ had compassion for people who were sick. He healed the sick and treated them with kindness. Healing was an important part of the ministry of Jesus Christ.

His actions showed others the great love that God has for all people. Jesus gave people hope. The healing miracles were a sign that God was present through Jesus Christ. We too are called to be people of compassion toward the sick.

WITH THE CHILDREN

Look up and discuss some of the following gospel stories about Jesus healing the sick.

Healing of a leper—Matthew 8:1–3

> ASK: WHY DID ONLY ONE LEPER SAY THANKS?

Healing a woman—Matthew 9:20–22

> ASK: HOW DO YOU THINK THE WOMAN FELT?

Healing a paralyzed man—Mark 2:1–12

> ASK: WHAT DOES IT MEAN TO BE PARALYZED?
> HOW DID THE MAN FEEL AFTERWARD?

Healing a man's hand—Luke 6:6–10

> ASK: HAVE YOU EVER BROKEN YOUR ARM OR HAND?

Healing a blind man—Luke 18:35–43

> ASK: HOW WOULD YOU FEEL IF YOU WERE BLIND
> AND JESUS HEALED YOU?

Healing an official's son—John 4:46–53

> ASK: WHAT DID THE MAN SAY TO JESUS?

Encourage the children (and their parents) to reach out to the sick in the parish, the community, and the world. Urge them to have compassion for those whose lives are challenged by illness. Talk about ways they can reach out to these people and help them at a time when they need a helping hand.

2 WALKING THROUGH THE RITE

BACKGROUND

Catholics celebrate the sacrament of the anointing of the sick in many places. The priest can go to the hospital, care center, or home of the person who is ill, elderly, facing surgery, or struggling with ongoing illness. Family and friends are invited to be part of the rite and may gather around the bed of their loved one.

The priest prays with the person who is ill and those who are present. He asks God for strength for the person who is ill. The priest places his hands on the head of the sick person. He anoints the person with blessed oil on the forehead and the hands with the sign of the cross. The anointing is for healing and strength.

Then everyone present prays the Our Father together. At the conclusion of the rite the priest gives a blessing to the person who is sick. He prays to God to bless the person who is ill and grant them hope and physical healing if possible.

Through anointing of the sick, the person who is ill and all present are comforted with the knowledge that God cares about us and is always with us. This sacrament can be received more than once even for the same illness if the person's condition is worse. The Church wants people to have the comfort of knowing that God is with them in their time of illness.

WITH THE CHILDREN

Walk through the rite of this sacrament with the children. Then ask them to pray for those who are sick, in the hospital, or in nursing homes. Gather the children in a circle and pray the Our Father together.

3 USING DISCUSSION QUESTIONS

BACKGROUND

Asking questions assures that children understand what has been explained and encourages discussion. Also questions help them personalize the information and see how to live it in their lives.

WITH THE CHILDREN

Following are some questions to share with children about the sacrament of anointing.

» Who can receive the sacrament of anointing?

» Can a person receive this sacrament more than once?

» Have you ever been to an anointing Mass or service?

» Is this sacrament only celebrated in a church?

» Why do we anoint people who are sick or elderly?

» Why does the priest make the sign of the cross with oil?

» What are ways we can help people who are sick or in a nursing home?

Also invite the children to ask their own questions or share their own thoughts. They often learn best from the answers and ideas of other children.

4

ASKING FAMILIES TO HELP

BACKGROUND

The sacrament of anointing is sometimes celebrated by Catholics within a healing Mass. Many parishes offer anointing Masses for their sick and elderly parishioners. Everyone is invited to participate in the liturgy whether they themselves are sick or not and to support those who are struggling with illness. Those who wish to receive the sacrament of anointing come forward during the Mass. This is a great way for a parish community to show support.

WITH THE CHILDREN

Encourage children to come with their families to a parish healing Mass. Invite them to take active roles such as greeting people, handing out worship aids, holding the door, and finding seats for people. Liturgical ministers are also needed for these Masses including altar servers and choir members. Some parishes also have a reception after an anointing Mass. People are needed to make cookies, put centerpieces on the tables, set up, serve refreshments, refill drinks, and clean up. Helping at an anointing Mass enables children to reach out to people who are sick in the parish with their words and actions.

5 DISCUSSING EXPERIENCES

BACKGROUND

It's always important for both children and adults to find ways to live what they learn. When they hear about helping the sick as Jesus did, they need to explore and apply this in their lives. Discussing specific scenarios helps children in particular explore how to help the sick in concrete ways.

WITH THE CHILDREN

Share the following scenarios with children and encourage their responses.

A boy in your class at school is sick and your teacher said that he won't be back for a while. What can you do?

A neighbor down the street just got out of the hospital and is using crutches to get around. What can you do?

You hear at church about an organization that helps children who are sick and need surgery. What can you do?

A girl in your school is blind and finds her way down the hall with a white cane. What can you do?

When you visit your grandma in the nursing home, you notice that some people don't have many visitors. What can you do?

6 LEARNING FROM ST. MARGUERITE D'YOUVILLE

BACKGROUND

The saints are examples for all of us of ways to serve God and other people. All of us benefit from hearing about those who lived their faith each day. St. Marguerite d'Youville was a compassionate person who lived in Canada and worked with the sick in hospitals. She was married and the mother of six children. Four of her children died when they were young. She took care of her sick husband until he died, even though he was a difficult man. She then became the head of a hospital in Montreal and fought for the right of the poor to medical care. She worked hard to see that the poor were not turned away when they needed help.

St. Marguerite was a courageous person who worked to make life better for those who were ill. She saw a need and did something about it. She made a difference in the lives of other people. She saw the face of Jesus in the poor and the sick. This Catholic saint is known as "the mother of universal charity." She shared God's love with everyone she met, even when life was difficult. She founded a religious order called the Sisters of Charity. They continue her work today in hospitals and nursing homes. St. Marguerite d'Youville is an example of how we are to care about the sick and other people in need.

WITH THE CHILDREN

Share the story of St. Marguerite d'Youville and then invite children to role play a visit to the hospital or the home of a sick person. They can choose whom they are visiting. Give them guidelines about how to greet the person, questions to ask, promises of prayer, and how to say goodbye. Remind them to remember the sick in their daily prayers.

7 MAKING CRAFT KITS

BACKGROUND

It is important to provide opportunities for children and families to reach out to those who are sick. A great service idea is making individual craft kits for a local children's hospital. Each kit contains all the supplies needed for one craft project along with easy directions. The craft kits can be packaged in one-gallon plastic storage bags. These kits can be used by children who are too sick to leave their beds to go to the hospital playroom. The craft projects provide something interesting for the children to do as they recuperate from illness or injury.

WITH THE CHILDREN

Ask the children and families to bring in supplies including colorful construction paper, manila drawing paper, glue sticks, children's safety scissors, markers, and gallon storage bags. Then work with them to assemble the craft kits. Be sure to include simple directions with each kit. Place everything needed for a single craft for an individual child in a plastic bag, along with the directions. Some crafts you can offer include:

Greeting cards: Put together folded construction paper and a box of markers to make greeting cards. The children can give these cards to parents, grandparents, nurses, doctors, and other children.

Drawing kits: Manila drawing paper and markers can be used to make pictures to decorate their room or give away to visitors.

Mosaic heart: Include a heart pattern, strips of colored construction paper, scissors, and a glue stick. Children make the mosaic heart by gluing squares of colorful construction paper to the heart. This project can be displayed in the child's hospital room to add a spot of bright color.

8 ADOPTING A GRANDPARENT

BACKGROUND

A great way for children to reach out to people who are sick or elderly is with an "Adopt a Grandparent" program at a nearby nursing home. In order to do this, the children need to be able to visit the nursing home several times during the year. Children pair up with individual residents to visit them and participate in activities such as bingo and birthday parties. This is a great way for children and their families to remember the sick and elderly all through the year. Check with the local nursing home about their requirements for such a project.

WITH THE CHILDREN

Invite someone from the nursing home or care center to talk with the children about working with the elderly. The children need to learn patience. They also must understand that sometimes people of any age can be difficult if they are not feeling well. Also practice possible scenarios with them before they visit a nursing home. Some people can't hear well; some are very feeble; some are not coherent. Also talk about people in wheelchairs, possible smells—anything that might startle or upset children.

9

OBSERVING WORLD DAY OF THE SICK

BACKGROUND

World Day of the Sick is observed on February 11, the Feast of Our Lady of Lourdes. This day reminds us to pray for the sick. The pope always issues a letter on this date about caring for the sick in the name of Jesus Christ. We are to open our eyes and our hearts to the needs of the sick around the world.

WITH THE CHILDREN

On or near this day encourage the children and their families to reach out to those who are sick in the parish and the community. Have them discuss ways to do this, such as a phone call, a greeting card, a bouquet of flowers, a book, a hot meal, or words of comfort. Also consider having a prayer service to offer prayer for the sick, the hospitalized, and the elderly. Encourage children to remember the sick around the world in their prayers each day. Ask their parents to support groups who reach out to the sick. There are many organizations, like Catholic Relief Services, that provide medical treatment for the poorest of the poor.

10 WRITING A LITANY

BACKGROUND

Praying for the sick is something all children can do every day. It is important for the children to learn to pray for the needs of others in addition to praying for their own needs. What happens to other people matters because we are all created in God's own image and likeness. As a community of God's people, we are called to pray for one another and care about one another, and especially for the sick.

One way to do this is to write a litany with the children. Ask them to name groups of people who are sick and need their prayers. Write down their suggestions.

WITH THE CHILDREN

Together pray the following litany for the sick with everyone responding, "Lord, hear our prayer."

Leader For people in the hospital, we pray…

All Lord, hear our prayer.

Leader For the elderly in nursing homes, we pray…

All Lord, hear our prayer.

Leader For people who live with disabilities, we pray…

All Lord, hear our prayer.

Leader For people who struggle with mental illness, we pray…

All Lord, hear our prayer.

Leader	For those facing long-term medical treatment, we pray...
All	Lord, hear our prayer.
Leader	For people who need surgery, we pray...
All	Lord, hear our prayer.
Leader	For all those who are sick and need our prayers, we pray...
All	Lord, hear our prayer.

HOLY ORDERS

Sacrament of Service

The sacrament of holy orders is a sacrament of service. On Holy Thursday Jesus washed the feet of his apostles and told them to do the same for others. As Jesus served others, so priests are called to serve the people of God in a special way. They are to witness to all that Jesus said and did. At Holy Thursday Mass we celebrate the service of the priesthood with a symbolic washing of the feet.

The bishop of a diocese ordains priests to serve the Catholic people of God in a special way through the sacrament of holy orders. Priests are anointed for service and called to preach the word of God. They are to be people of hope who are with us on our faith journey to the Father. Their call is to help people live as followers of Jesus Christ.

After his resurrection, Jesus told his disciples to continue his mission to the world so that the gospel would be proclaimed to people of all nations and all generations. All of us share in that mission. Jesus sent us the Holy Spirit to help us do this. Each of us has a vocation to serve God and other people in God's name. We should encourage children to pray and reflect on what their vocation might be and how they will live it out in their lives. Following are ways for children and their families to learn about the sacrament of holy orders. Ideas are also included to help them learn that each of us has a vocation and is called by God to service.

1

DISPLAYING SYMBOLS OF HOLY ORDERS

BACKGROUND

To engage the children's interest and attention set up symbols of Holy Orders and the priesthood in the church. Put out a vestment, the book of the gospels, a sacramentary with the Mass prayers, a chalice, a paten, and other things that a priest uses in service to the people. This might also include a diocesan pamphlet about vocations. Set up the objects on and near the presider's chair.

WITH THE CHILDREN

Take the children to the church and talk about Holy Orders and some of the ways Catholic priests are asked to serve others. This includes

» celebrating Mass,

» being pastor of a parish,

» working as chaplains in hospitals,

» teaching in high schools and colleges,

» doing missionary work far from home.

Ask children what other things the priests in their parish do to offer service.

2 WRITING TO SEMINARIANS

BACKGROUND

Explain to children that when someone feels the call to be a priest, he enters a seminary to study, learn, and pray. The person may just have finished high school or may have had a career before deciding to be a priest. Let the children know that it takes years to prepare before the person is ordained a priest.

After he receives the sacrament of holy orders, a new priest is assigned to help in a parish, school, hospital, or other ministry. Some priests become associate pastors in a parish, others may be hospital chaplains, others are teachers or missionaries, some work in diocesan offices, and still others are involved in a variety of ministries that serve God and other people.

WITH THE CHILDREN

Talk to the children about the seminarians in your diocese who are preparing to be ordained. There are usually several men in different stages of formation for the priesthood. This information is readily available from the diocesan vocations office.

Give children paper and pencils and invite them to write to one of the seminarians as a show of support. Remind them and their families to pray for the people who are preparing to become priests. The seminarians are happy to receive mail from the children and to know that people are thinking of them and praying for them as they prepare to receive the sacrament of Holy Orders.

3 MAKING VOCATION POSTERS

BACKGROUND

Do some research about the work of various orders of priests, brothers, sisters, and other people involved in ministry. Some of these ministries include hospitals, schools, homeless shelters, missions, and clinics.

Gather pictures from as many sources as possible including mission magazines, Catholic magazines, various religious orders, your diocesan vocation office, and the web. Have poster board, markers, scissors, glue sticks, and construction paper available.

WITH THE CHILDREN

First ask children to gather in small groups and decide on a title for their posters. This might be something like "Vocations" or "Serving the people of God." Then have them cut out the pictures they want to use. They can back each picture with a slightly larger piece of colored construction paper to form a frame. When they like the arrangement of the items on their posters, they can glue the pictures and frames in place. They can also write words on their posters such as "great work," "wow," or "amazing."

When they are finished, each group can show their poster to the other groups and tell about it. Be sure to display these posters in the hallway where everyone can see them and learn more about vocations.

4 INVITING A VOCATION SPEAKER

BACKGROUND

Ask a speaker to come to the children's session and speak to them about vocations. Many diocesan offices have a vocations office, and the director of vocations is often available to go out to parishes and schools to speak to children about vocations to the priesthood and religious life and about "vocations" in general.

WITH THE CHILDREN

Talk to children beforehand about how each of us has a vocation. Invite them to listen to the visitor with polite attention. Allow the opportunity for them to ask questions of the speaker. Questions might include: How did you know that you had a vocation to the priesthood or religious life? What are some of the things you do in your ministry? What do you like best about being a priest or religious sister? Why is it important to pray for vocations? What can I do if I think I might be interested in becoming a priest or religious? What are some other ways to serve God?

5 WALKING THROUGH THE RITE

BACKGROUND

The bishop of a diocese is the one who ordains men to the priesthood because he is their leader and teacher, the chief "shepherd" of the diocese. The ordination ceremony usually takes place in the cathedral, the mother church of the diocese.

Following are three aspects of the rite of ordination.

- *Election of candidates.* In the first part of the rite, a witness for each person to be ordained speaks of how the person has prepared for ordination. In many cases the witness is from the seminary. During the homily the bishop reflects on the readings and talks about the qualities needed by these candidates.

- *Promise of the elect.* Through a series of questions, the candidates express their desire to work with the bishop, preach the Word of God, celebrate the sacraments, be people of prayer, and follow Christ. In the promise of the elect they are reminded that Jesus came not to be served, but to serve others.

- *Litany of the saints.* After praying to the saints, the bishop places his hands on each candidate, symbolizing the outpouring of the Holy Spirit. The bishop may remind those to be ordained that gifts are to be shared. The hands of the newly ordained priests are anointed with oil. This is a reminder of their sacred duties to offer the Eucharist and serve the people of God.

WITH THE CHILDREN

Ask the children if any of them have ever been to an ordination. If yes, ask what they remember. Briefly share with them the three items above, focusing on the litany of the saints. Explain that priests, like the children themselves, need the prayers of Mary and the saints to follow Jesus faithfully. Pray a brief litany of saints with them by praying to their "name saints." All can answer: Pray for us.

6
EXPLORING THE CALL OF THE APOSTLES

BACKGROUND

Each of us is called to follow Jesus Christ in our lives and so we too are apostles. Read Matthew 4:18–20 and think about how this gospel speaks to you in your ministry.

WITH THE CHILDREN

Read the above gospel with the children. Then have them answer and discuss these questions:

» Where was Jesus walking in this story?

» What were Peter and Andrew doing?

» What did Jesus say to these fishermen and what did they do?

» What were James and John doing and what did they do when Jesus called them?

» How does this story speak to you?

» Are you too called to follow Jesus?

» What are some ways that you can follow Jesus? (Offer hints like helping the poor, sharing the good news with others, visiting the sick, giving food to the food pantry, and working for peace and justice in our world.)

7

LEARNING FROM ST. JOHN BOSCO

BACKGROUND

St. John Bosco lived in Italy and as a young man he learned how to juggle and do magic tricks. When he became a Catholic priest, he continued put on shows for children. He was an outgoing person and people gathered around him. His heart was moved especially by the poor orphans who had nowhere to go. He found a place for them to stay and helped them learn a trade so they would not have to steal to eat. St. John Bosco is the patron saint of young people everywhere. He founded a religious order called the Salesians. They continue his work of helping orphans and homeless children in countries around the world. They staff orphanages, clinics, feeding programs, schools, and shelters that minister to children in need.

WITH THE CHILDREN

Share the story of St. John Bosco. Then ask the children if they think there are still children who need our help today. Share some examples: homeless children in Haiti, refugee children in Darfur and Palestine, etc.

ACTIVITY

8 LEARNING ABOUT RELIGIOUS SISTERS

BACKGROUND

Some women choose to serve God by being sisters in a religious order. Although they do not receive the sacrament of Holy Orders, they commit themselves totally to a lifetime of service to others. Sisters come from many different backgrounds. They are involved in many different ministries to serve the people of God around the world, and they bring hope to people in difficult circumstances. They help the poor and the sick. There are many religious orders of sisters. You might want to explore some of these orders and share the information with the children.

WITH THE CHILDREN

If possible, invite a religious sister to visit the children to talk about her life and her work. Encourage children to ask questions about how they can do the work of the gospel themselves in small daily ways.

9 FOCUSING ON VOCATIONS FOR ALL

BACKGROUND

All of us have a vocation. God calls each of us to a life of holiness and service with Jesus Christ as our example. Some people are called to the priesthood or religious life and other people are called to minister in a variety of other ways.

WITH THE CHILDREN

Ask the children to think about how God might be calling them. Let them know that God calls each of them in many unique and different ways. Sometimes God speaks to their hearts in prayer and sometimes God calls to them through other people. Encourage the children to examine their God-given gifts and talents and abilities and see how they could share these gifts with others. Encourage them to look into their hearts and see where God is leading them. They should ask themselves, "How is God calling me?"

10 PRAYING FOR VOCATIONS

BACKGROUND

Encourage children and their families to pray for vocations with a prayer like the following:

> God, Father and Creator,
> we pray for all those you have chosen
> to serve you as a priest, brother, or sister.
> Be with them and guide them
> that they may faithfully serve the people of God.
> We pray that more people
> will answer your call to become priests, brothers,
>   and sisters.
> We pray that we too will know our vocation
> and live it in our lives each day.
> May we share the gifts and talents
> we have been given with others.
> Help us to hear your call and to follow your way
> wherever that leads us.
> Amen.

MATRIMONY

Sacrament of Commitment

In the sacrament of matrimony a man and woman make promises to each other and to God. They commit themselves to be faithful to each other, even when times are difficult. They pledge to love each other for the rest of their lives. The Catholic priest who celebrates the sacrament of matrimony is a witness to their marriage vows and gives the couple the blessing of the Church.

Marriage is an important vocation. In marriage a man and woman support one another in living Spirit-filled lives. It is important for the children to understand that this is a sacrament that takes much preparation for couples to live a lifetime together. They need to see that preparing for marriage is about more than just planning the celebration. Be sensitive to children whose parents are not married in the church or who are divorced.

People who are married are called to share God's love with each other and with their children. They are the first teachers of their children in the ways of faith. Our faith in God must be lived in our everyday lives as a family. Encourage families to participate in Mass each week and serve others in their daily lives. Encourage families to pray together at home, to forgive one another as the need arises, and to support one another. Let them know that families are not called to be perfect, but they are called to be faithful followers of Jesus Christ.

Families should nurture the faith of their children and help them grow in love of God and others. Families must share with one another the gift of hope in God and hope in the future. Following are some activities to help children and families explore the sacrament of matrimony. Ideas are also included to help families share their faith together and live it in their daily lives.

1

SHARING A SYMBOL TABLE

BACKGROUND

This sacrament is a celebration of the love and commitment of two people who declare their vows before God, the Church, and one another. A couple asks God's blessing on their union and on their future.

Some symbols of marriage include a framed wedding picture, a worship aid from a nuptial Mass, a Bible open to 1 Corinthians 13:4–7, a pamphlet about pre-marriage preparation, a picture of wedding rings, and a wedding invitation.

WITH THE CHILDREN

Set up a display with some or all of these symbols on it. Note which items engage the interest and attention of the children. A wedding picture usually is something that catches their eye. This symbol table provides a visual focus when talking about the sacrament of matrimony. Invite them to ask questions about the symbols. Let them know, for example, that the rings symbolize the promises that the couple makes.

2 WALKING THROUGH THE RITE

BACKGROUND

The important part of a wedding day is the sacrament and not the reception that follows it. It is at the church that the couple pledges to be faithful to each other for a lifetime and are united in marriage.

WITH THE CHILDREN

In the sacrament of matrimony, the couple declares consent to the marriage by saying "I do." Then the priest blesses the rings and the couple puts them on as a sign of love and faithfulness. The rings remind them of the sacrament that they have received and the vocation they are to live for a lifetime. Invite children to take turns role playing this part of the rite. The "priest" blesses the rings, "In the name of the Father and of the Son and of the Holy Spirit." The couple says "Amen" and puts them on.

Explain that the nuptial blessing takes place after the Lord's prayer. The priest asks everyone present to pray that God will bless the man and woman so that they will be faithful witnesses of Christ in the way they lives their lives. After Mass the couple goes forth in hope for the future as they begin their married life together. Now invite the children to recite the Our Father together for all the couples who will soon celebrate the sacrament of marriage.

3

INVITING A MARRIED COUPLE

BACKGROUND

The sacrament of matrimony is for a lifetime. Couples preparing for marriage are prepared by focusing on the ceremony itself and the promises of love and fidelity. Marriage preparation is more than planning a big party.

Ask a married couple to come and speak to the children about what marriage means. This can be the parents of one of the children or a sponsor couple who is involved in marriage preparation. Ask the couple to describe what marriage means to them and talk about what it takes to have a good marriage. The speakers may also want to talk about staying together through the good times and the bad times.

WITH THE CHILDREN

Having a speaker makes a lesson on this sacrament come alive for the children. It is a great way to show them marriage in action. Many of them may not have had this experience in their own families, so speakers provide a positive example of marriage. Encourage the children to ask any questions that they may have.

4 LEARNING FROM ELIZABETH OF HUNGARY

BACKGROUND

This saint was a princess because her father was King of Hungary. She married and had three children. She chose to live a life of service to others, especially the poor and sick. Day after day she brought food to the hungry. Her husband supported her in all that she did, even when there was criticism from other wealthy people. Later her husband, whom she loved dearly, died, and she became a widow. She still carried on her good works. Her life reminds all of us that Jesus calls us to love others.

WITH THE CHILDREN

Children need to have examples of what it means to live a vocation to the married life. Within that vocation are many opportunities to serve God and others in the parish and in the community. Share with them the example of St. Elizabeth of Hungary. Then encourage them to bring in non-perishable food items for the parish food pantry.

5

DISCUSSING THE PREPARATION

BACKGROUND

Preparing for the sacrament of matrimony is about more than planning a wedding. Important topics must be discussed by a couple before marriage, for example: how they will raise their children, how to handle money, and how to get along with in-laws. The engaged couple should talk about their expectation of marriage in all areas, including how they will handle disagreements. All couples and families have difficulties sometimes. They must listen to one another and support one another during trying times. Couples should bring hope to each other in times of sadness and celebrate together in times of joy.

WITH THE CHILDREN

Ask questions to promote discussion about the sacrament of matrimony.

» Why do you think couples have to prepare for marriage?

» What are some of the things people should talk about before getting married?

» Why do couples exchange rings at their wedding?

Also invite children to ask their questions about this sacrament.

6 EXPLORING FAMILY LIFE

BACKGROUND

Raising children to be faithful followers of Jesus Christ is an important part of being married and having a family. The U.S. Bishops wrote a pastoral message to families called *Follow the Way of Love*. The bishops stress that families are a sign of God's presence in the world. They remind us that all of us, whether married, single, or ordained, share a common vocation to follow Jesus Christ in our daily lives.

Families are called to believe in God and share their faith as a family. Parents are the primary teachers of their children about how to live in love as followers of Jesus Christ. Families should pray together, forgive one another, and serve others in the name of Jesus Christ. Families are called the domestic church. Each family and each generation is called to make a difference in the world. Family life can be a challenge, but love binds family members together.

WITH THE CHILDREN

Give them a piece of drawing paper and ask each to draw the members of their family or extended family and name them. Have them write these words at the bottom of the drawing: "Jesus loves my family."

7

COLLECTING ITEMS FOR A SHELTER

BACKGROUND

Families must be encouraged to open their hearts to other families in time of hardship. One way to do this is to collect items needed by the local shelter for families who are homeless. These shelters give the family a safe place to stay while they get back on their feet. Let the children and families know about the family shelter, the people they serve, and what is provided.

These shelters are always in need of items for the families they serve. The families not only need supplies while they are staying at the shelter, but they need items to set up housekeeping once they move on to other housing.

WITH THE CHILDREN

Invite children (with their parents) to collect supplies such as the following: towels, glasses, dishes, silverware, pots and pans, toothpaste, toothbrushes, soap, laundry soap, stamps, light bulbs, paper towels, paper plates and cups, diapers, coffee, tea, and non-perishable food. Have them bring the items to a designated place for packing and invite one or two families to join you when you deliver the supplies.

Also give families information about the shelter and other needs such as evening meals, lawn care, painting, and other ways they might be of service. Encourage them to be involved on an ongoing basis. The need is great.

8

ENCOURAGING PARTICIPATION AT MASS

BACKGROUND

Couples and families are called to worship God together each week by participating in Sunday Mass. The Mass is the communal prayer of the Church and attending as a family is part of the commitment of marriage. It is part of living the Catholic faith.

As we come together at Mass, we offer God all that we have done during the week and everything that has happened to us. We listen to God speak to us in the scriptures. We offer praise and thanksgiving to God in the Eucharist. Strengthened by the Eucharist we go forward to again become all that God has created us to be for the world. All that we do during the week should flow from our experience of Sunday Mass.

Many parishes now have a question of the week based on the Sunday readings. This helps families "break open the Word" of scripture. This question can be discussed at home as families share their faith and live that faith in their daily lives.

WITH THE CHILDREN

Remind them of the importance of Mass as part of family life. Then ask and discuss the following:

» How does going to Mass help your family?

» Do you ever talk about the readings or the homily on the way home?

» How does the Mass help you to be a better person?

» How does the Mass help you to be closer to God in your life?